T0197613

Right Left: A Boy Named Grey

Match your Left and Right hands to those hidden on each page.

《左与右，叫小灰的男孩》

找到每页隐藏的左手和右手.

Author: Leslie Moore

作者：莱斯利·摩尔

Chinese Translation: Ziheng Zhu

中文翻译：朱子恒

WestBow Press books may be ordered through booksellers or by contacting:

WestBow Press
A Division of Thomas Nelson & Zondervan
1663 Liberty Drive
Bloomington, IN 47403
www.westbowpress.com
844-714-3454

ISBN: 978-1-4497-8649-6 (sc)
ISBN: 978-1-4497-8653-3 (e)

Library of Congress Control Number: 2013903633

Print information available on the last page.

WestBow Press rev. date: 02/23/2021

WestBow
PRESS®
A DIVISION OF THOMAS NELSON
& ZONDERVAN

Hello Friend, my name is Grey.
I live with my Father, Mother, and Cat "Orange".
Orange is a mellow little fellow.

大家好,我的名字是小灰。
我和我爸爸,妈妈还有一只叫做橙色的猫住在一起。
橙色是可爱的小家伙。

Right now I'm an only child, but not for long.
Mom is going to have another baby.
Soon I will have a brother or sister.

My family is growing.

虽然我现在是家里的独生子，但情况马上就不一样了。
因为妈妈即将有第二个宝宝。
很快我就会有一个弟弟或者妹妹了。

我的家庭在茁壮成长。

To the left of us live the Shells.
The Shells have lots and lots of grandchildren.

我们家左边住的是贝壳家。
贝壳家有很多很多的小孩。

To the right of us lives my Uncle Blue,
Aunt Red, and their daughter Purple.

Uncle Blue's name suits him well because
he jams night and day to the blues.

我们右边住得是我的蓝叔叔，红婶婶，
和他们的女儿小紫。

蓝叔叔的名字非常的适合他，
因为他每天从早到晚都在玩儿蓝调。

When I am not playing with the little Shells or listening to my Uncle Blue's jam session, I enjoy:

- Riding my bike
- Reading
- Playing soccer
- And believe it or not, helping my mom vacuum around the house.

当我不是在和小贝壳玩耍或是听我蓝叔叔即兴演奏爵士乐的时候，我喜欢：

- 骑自行车
- 读书
- 踢足球
- 或许你不信，我还会帮我妈妈打扫房间。

All kids have differences; however, we have much more in common. For Instance do you:

- Giggle when you are tickled?
- Scratch when you are itchy?
- Cry when you are hurt?
- Smile when you are happy?

虽然每个小孩都很独特, 但我们还是有很多共同点的。比如说, 你会不会:

- 被挠痒时大笑?
- 发痒时抓自己?
- 伤心时哭泣?
- 高兴时欢笑?

LIBRARY

Most kids:

- Go to school
- Enjoy going to a birthday party
- Join their Public library
- Have a special hobby.

多数小孩都会:

- 去上学
- 喜欢去生日聚会
- 去图书馆
- 有独特的爱好。

People have favorite foods, such as spaghetti and meatballs, strawberries, and ice cream...YUM!

And everyone has to eat.

每人都有最爱吃的食物，我最喜欢的是意大利面牛肉圆，草莓，和冰淇淋 ... YUM!

People have a lot in common:

- Family, pets, and neighbors
- Interests, such as reading and playing soccer
- Laughing and giggling
- Favorite foods to eat.

大家其实有很多共同点的 :

- 家 , 宠物 , 邻居
- 读书和踢足球之类的兴趣爱好
- 开心的大笑或者傻笑
- 最爱吃的东西。

What do you think friend?
Do we have anything in common?
I bet we do!

所以, 朋友们 , 你们觉得呢？
我们有共同点吗？
我打赌我们有！

Coloring Pages

涂彩页

Hello Friend, my name is Grey.

I live with my Father, Mother, and Cat "Orange".

Orange is a mellow little fellow.

大家好,我的名字是小灰。

我和我爸爸,妈妈还有一只叫做橙色的猫住在一起。

橙色是可爱的小家伙。

Right now I'm an only child, but not for long.
Mom is going to have another baby.
Soon I will have a brother or sister.

My family is growing.

虽然我现在是家里的独生子, 但情况马上就不一样了。
因为妈妈即将有第二个宝宝。
很快我就会有一个弟弟或者妹妹了。

我的家庭在茁壮成长。

To the left of us live the Shells.
The Shells have lots and lots of grandchildren.

我们家左边住的是贝壳家。
贝壳家有很多很多的小孩。

To the right of us lives my Uncle Blue, Aunt Red, and their daughter Purple.

Uncle Blue's name suits him well because he jams night and day to the blues.

我们右边住得是我的蓝叔叔，红婶婶，和他们的女儿小紫。

蓝叔叔的名字非常的适合他，因为他每天从早到晚都在玩儿蓝调。

STAND-UP BASS

TRUMPET

TROMBONE

PIANO

SAXOPHONE

DRUM SET

CLARINET

GUITAR

When I am not playing with the little Shells or listening to my Uncle Blue's jam session, I enjoy:

- Riding my bike
- Reading
- Playing soccer
- And believe it or not, helping my mom vacuum around the house.

当我不是在和小贝壳玩耍或是听我蓝叔叔即兴演奏爵士乐的时候，我喜欢：

- 骑自行车
- 读书
- 踢足球
- 或许你不信，我还会帮我妈妈打扫房间。

All kids have differences; however, we have much more in common. For Instance do you:

- Giggle when you are tickled?
- Scratch when you are itchy?
- Cry when you are hurt?
- Smile when you are happy?

虽然每个小孩都很独特, 但我们还是有很多共同点的。比如说, 你会不会：

- 被挠痒时大笑？
- 发痒时抓自己？
- 伤心时哭泣？
- 高兴时欢笑？

Most kids:

- Go to school
- Enjoy going to a birthday party
- Join their Public library
- Have a special hobby.

多数小孩都会:
- 去上学
- 喜欢去生日聚会
- 去图书馆
- 有独特的爱好。

LIBRARY

People have favorite foods, such as spaghetti and meatballs, strawberries, and ice cream...YUM!

And everyone has to eat.

每人都有最爱吃的食物, 我最喜欢的是意大利面牛肉圆, 草莓, 和冰淇淋 ... YUM!

People have a lot in common:

- Family, pets, and neighbors
- Interests, such as reading and playing soccer
- Laughing and giggling
- Favorite foods to eat.

大家其实有很多共同点的：

- 家，宠物，邻居
- 读书和踢足球之类的兴趣爱好
- 开心的大笑或者傻笑
- 最爱吃的东西。

What do you think friend?
Do we have anything in common?
I bet we do!

所以，朋友们，你们觉得呢？
我们有共同点吗？
我打赌我们有！

Printed in the United States
by Baker & Taylor Publisher Services